The Test Tutor™

Practice Test
for the
Woodcock Johnson®-III
Tests of Cognitive Abilities

STUDENT BOOKLET

Test Tutor Publishing, LLC

TABLE OF CONTENTS

1

2

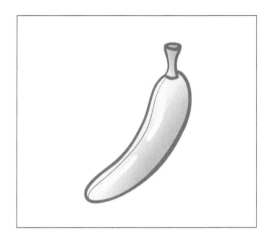

3

4

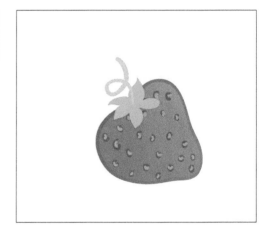

5

6

7

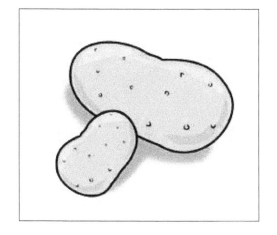

8

9

10

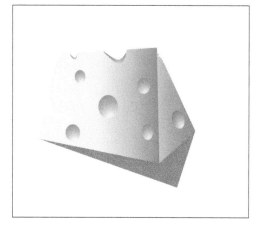

11

12

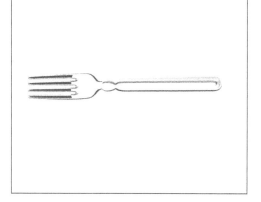

13

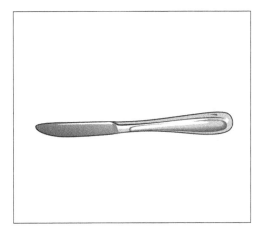

14

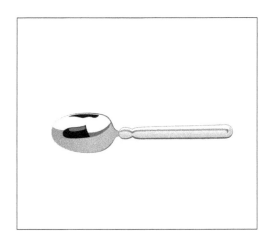

15

16

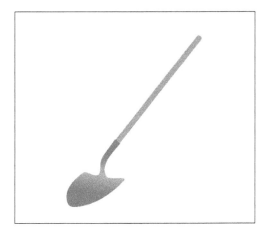

17

18

19

20

21

22

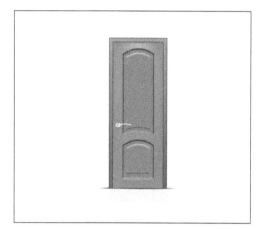

23

24

25

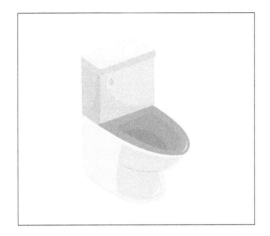

26

27

28

29

30

31

32

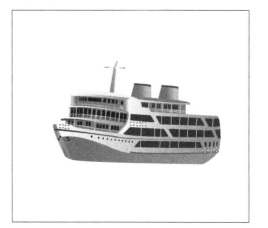

33

34

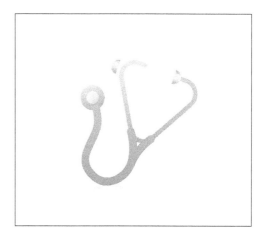

35

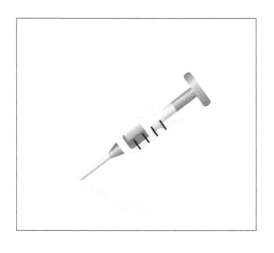

36

Happy

Sad

Big

Smart

Pretty

Shy

Automobile

Polite

Deceitful

Radiant

Fierce

Irrational

Artificial

Ancient

Generous

Authentic

Go

Long

Open

Big

Woman

Smooth

Flat

Good

Them

Young

Fast

Night

Rich

Black

Sharp

Commence

Conceal

Obvious

Ambiguous

Nose : Smell   Mouth:

Shoes: Wear   Food:

Shirt: Cloth   Window:

Ring: Finger   Scarf:

On: Off   Go:

Rabbit: Fast   Turtle:

Yes: No   Soft:

Big: Large   Small:

Frog: Jump   Bird:

River: Sky   Fish:

Street: Lake   Bus:

Telephone: Pencil   Talk:

Elbow: Knee   Wrist:

Ball: Can   Sphere:

1

2

3

4

5

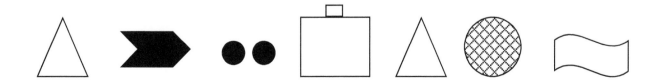

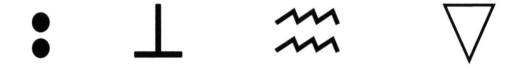

6

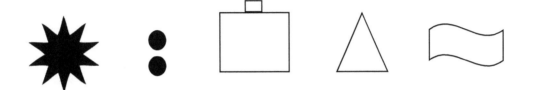

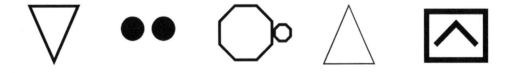

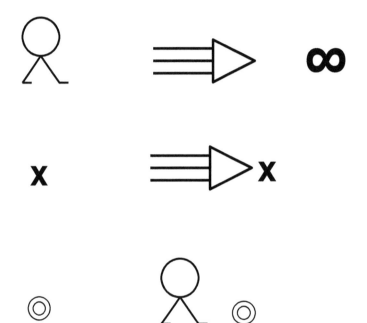

7

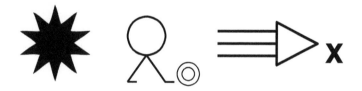

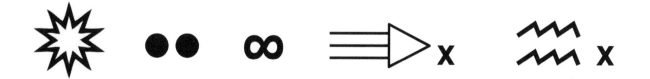

1

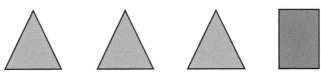

2

3

4

5

6

7

8

9
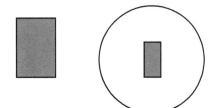

10
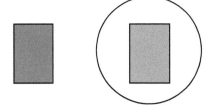

11
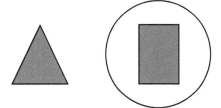

12

13

14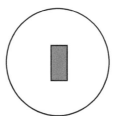

15

16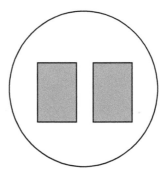

17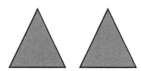

18

19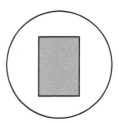

20

21

22

23

24

25

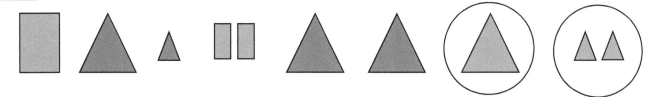

26

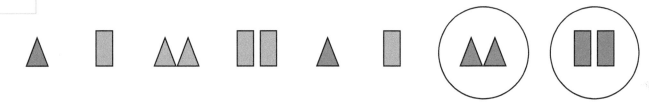

27

28

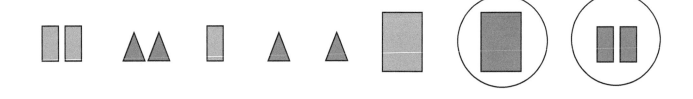

29

30

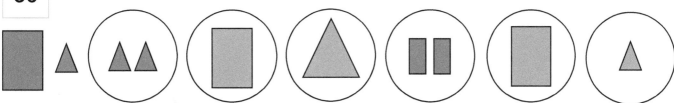

31

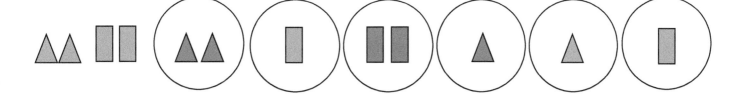

32

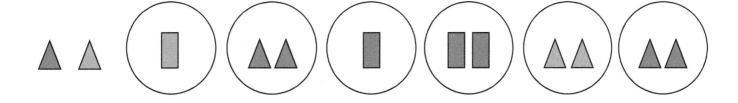

33

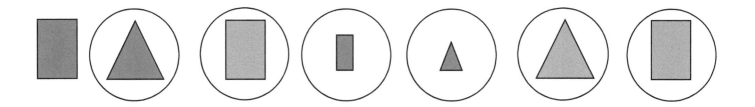

34

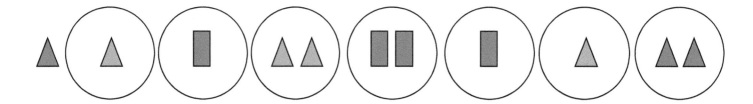

35

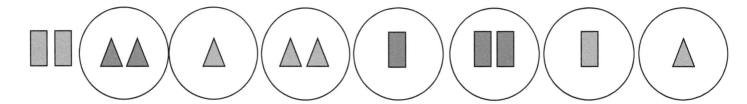

36

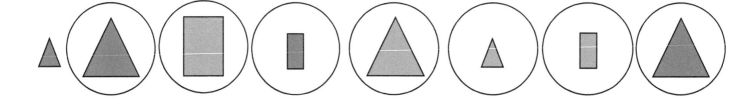

37

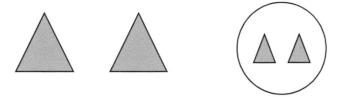

38

39

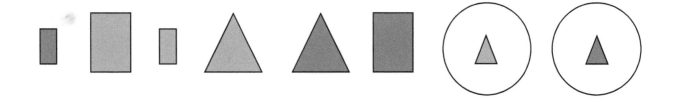

40

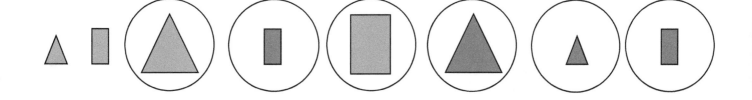

Concept Formation

41

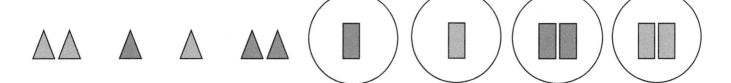

42

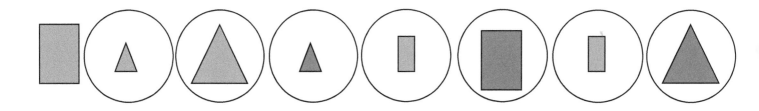

43

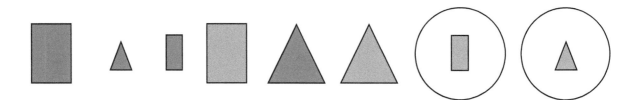

44

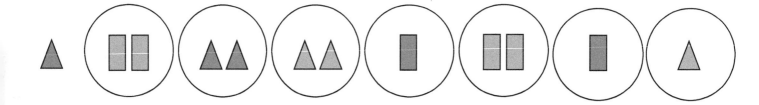

45

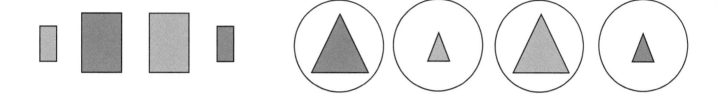

46

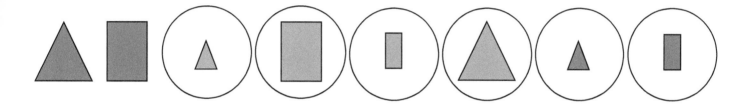

47

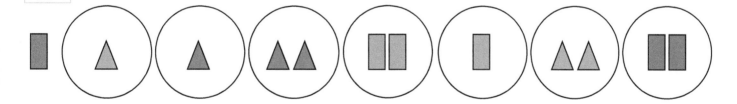

Practice Exercises

S	P	J	G	P	B
D	M	D	R	T	H

A	B	C	B	D	F
C	S	M	L	U	M
V	V	B	Y	T	R
J	C	M	Y	V	Y
E	W	A	S	A	Z
X	W	O	W	N	M
Z	D	B	S	T	D
R	I	U	R	V	Q
X	P	O	B	C	X
B	V	Z	T	T	E
L	A	Z	E	D	Z
B	B	A	V	F	T
V	F	H	C	F	Y
G	W	I	I	O	U
J	S	V	B	I	V
H	V	C	L	X	L
U	O	U	P	B	C
X	H	Y	T	H	M
P	W	H	T	P	S
I	H	K	E	X	K

CV	AC	VC	VA	AC	AV
UF	FO	FU	UF	UE	UM
HS	ZH	SH	ZK	SH	HZ
TE	NT	TN	NF	FN	TN
WN	WM	MW	WM	WV	WY
AD	AO	DA	AD	OV	OA
MV	VI	IV	VM	WM	MV
XH	JT	IK	TJ	VJ	JT
MG	GH	GM	GM	MS	MF
DE	DE	DF	DB	DV	DC
GL	LZ	LG	LS	LG	GP
SZ	XS	XZ	SX	SX	SK
ZI	IZ	ZK	ZV	ZI	IU
QR	BR	RR	RB	KR	BR
GC	FG	GF	FO	GF	CG
DY	JD	DN	JD	JB	DG
RR	KR	BR	PR	MR	RR
KH	BH	BH	HB	KB	BP
YZ	ZY	XY	ZX	VX	YZ
KM	MK	RN	MR	RM	RM

ABC	ACB	BAC	ACB	CBA	BCA
FBJ	BJF	FBJ	JFB	FJB	BFJ
SCR	RCS	CRS	SRC	CRS	RSC
TDL	DLT	LTD	LDT	TLD	LDT
HGO	GOH	HGO	GHO	OHG	OGH
QME	EQM	MEQ	EMQ	EQM	MQE
XUN	UNX	XNU	UXN	NUX	XUN
IZY	ZIY	IYZ	IYZ	YIZ	ZYI
TQP	TPQ	PQT	TPQ	QTP	QPT
UOP	OPU	OUP	POU	OUP	PUO
MAH	MHA	AHM	MAH	AMH	HMA
NMW	MNW	MWN	WMN	NWM	WMN
XCR	RXC	CRX	RCX	RXC	CXR
KDT	KTD	TKD	DKT	KDT	TDK
SPV	PSV	VPS	SVP	PVS	VPS
FDH	DHF	DFH	FHD	DFH	HFD
SIH	ISH	SHI	ISH	HIS	IHS
NJZ	ZNJ	JZN	ZJN	JNZ	NJZ
WUC	UCW	WUC	CWU	UWC	CUW
ZSY	SYZ	YZS	ZYS	YSZ	ZYS

Completion Time: _____

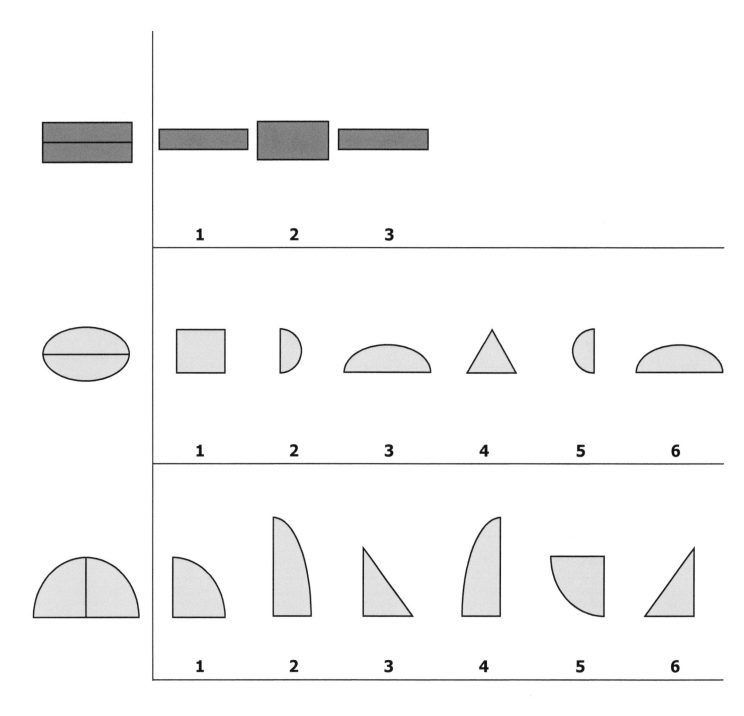

1   2   3

1   2   3   4   5   6

1   2   3   4   5   6

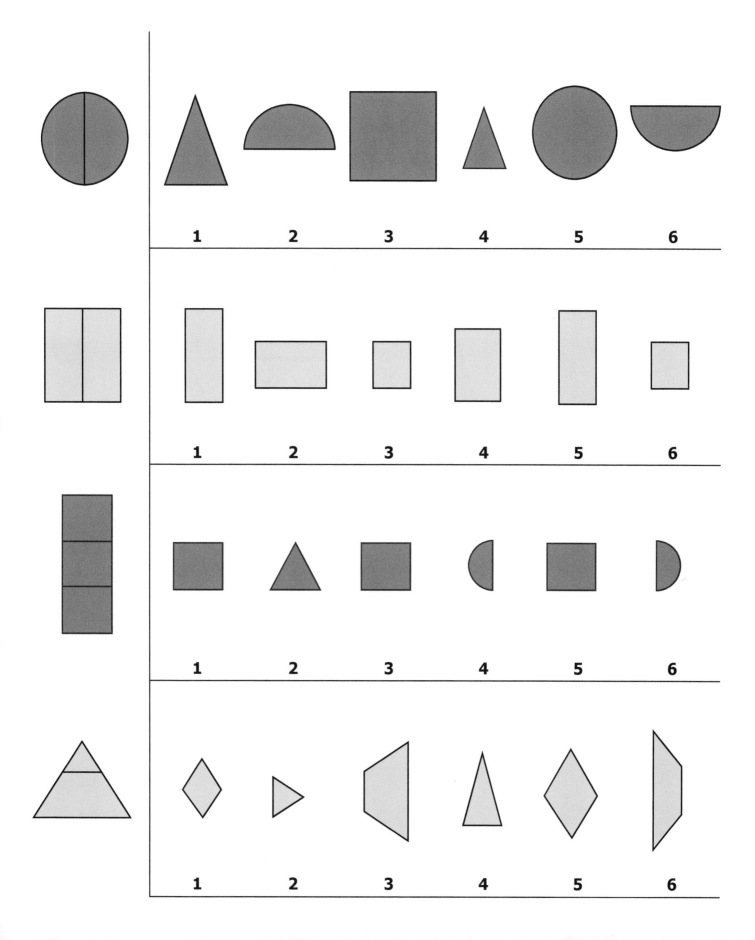

1   2   3   4   5   6

1   2   3   4   5   6

1   2   3   4   5   6

1   2   3   4   5   6

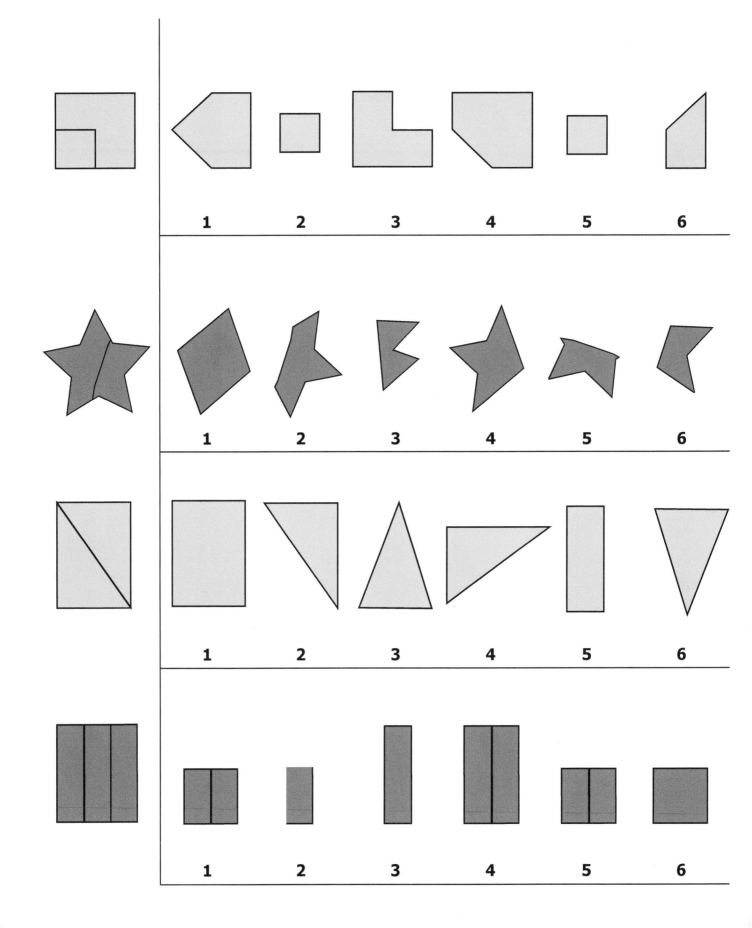

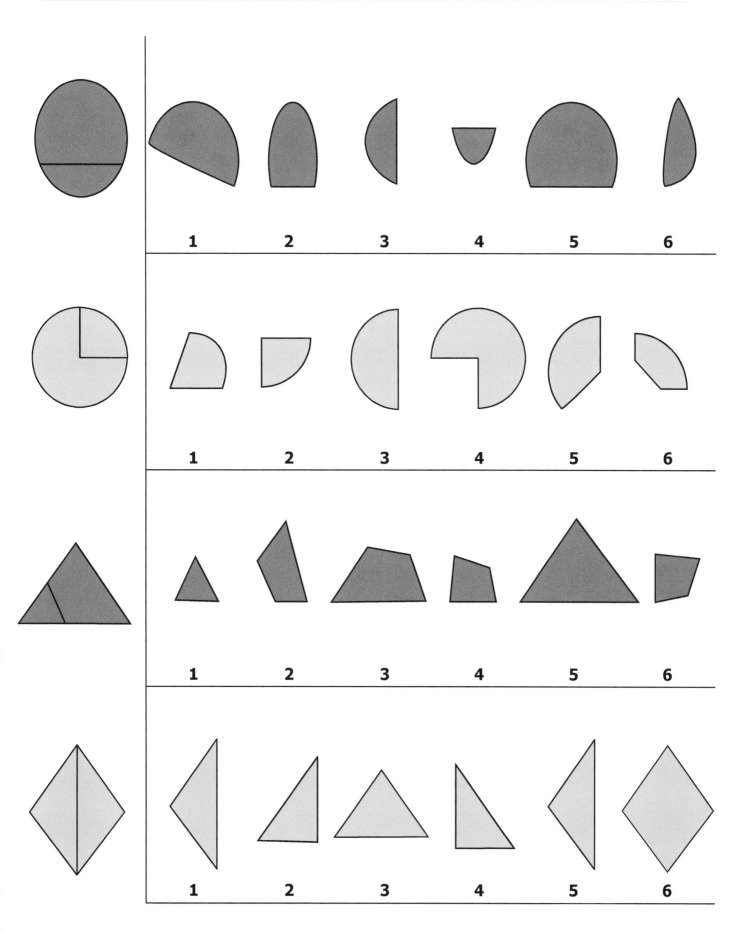

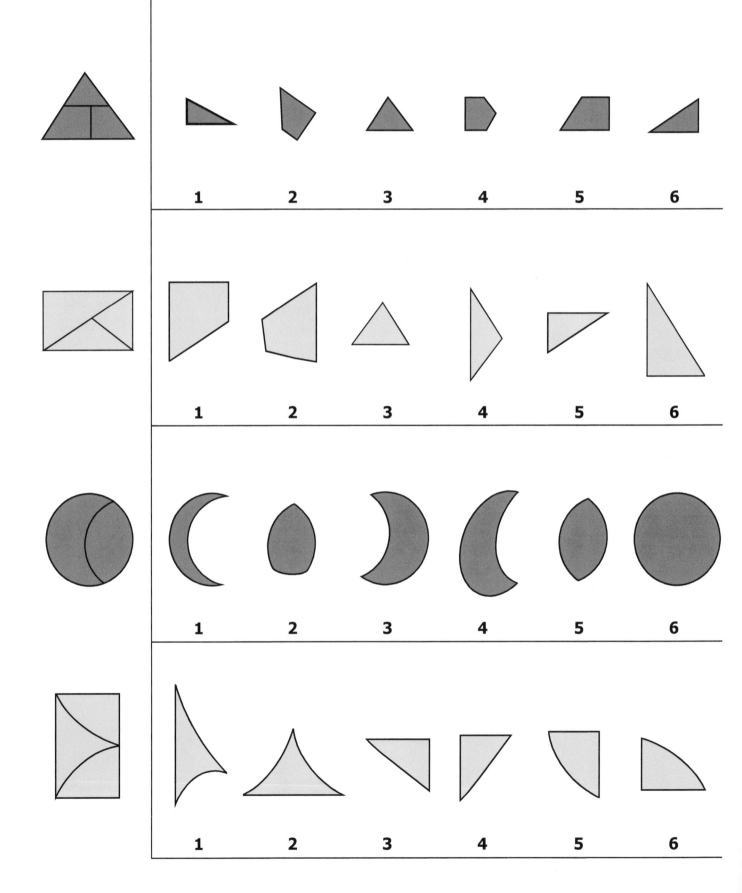

1 2 3 4 5 6

1 2 3 4 5 6

1 2 3 4 5 6

1 2 3 4 5 6

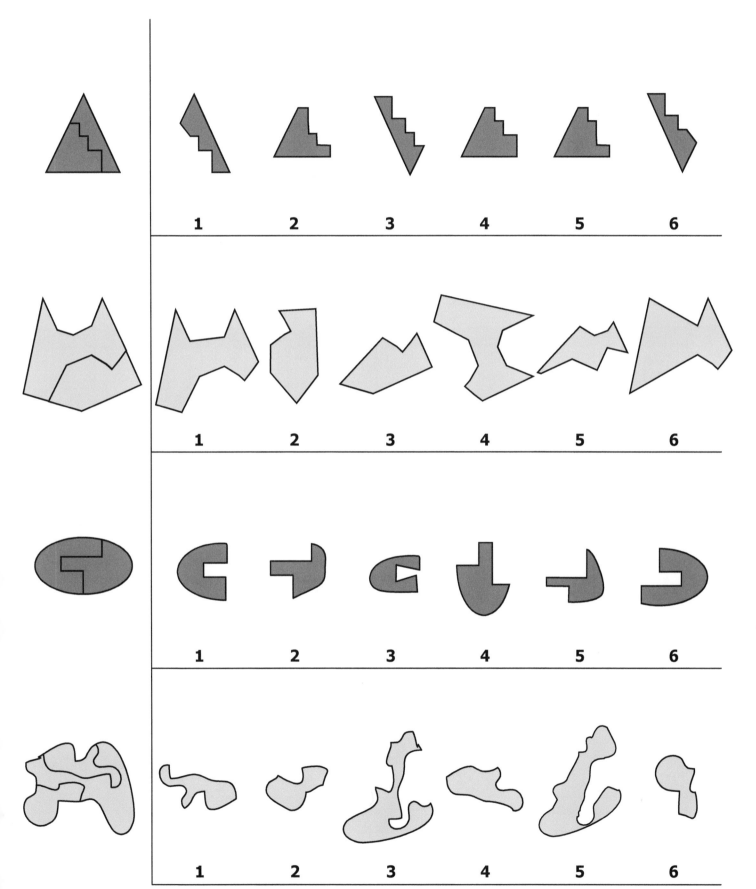

1   2   3   4   5   6

1   2   3   4   5   6

1   2   3   4   5   6

1   2   3   4   5   6

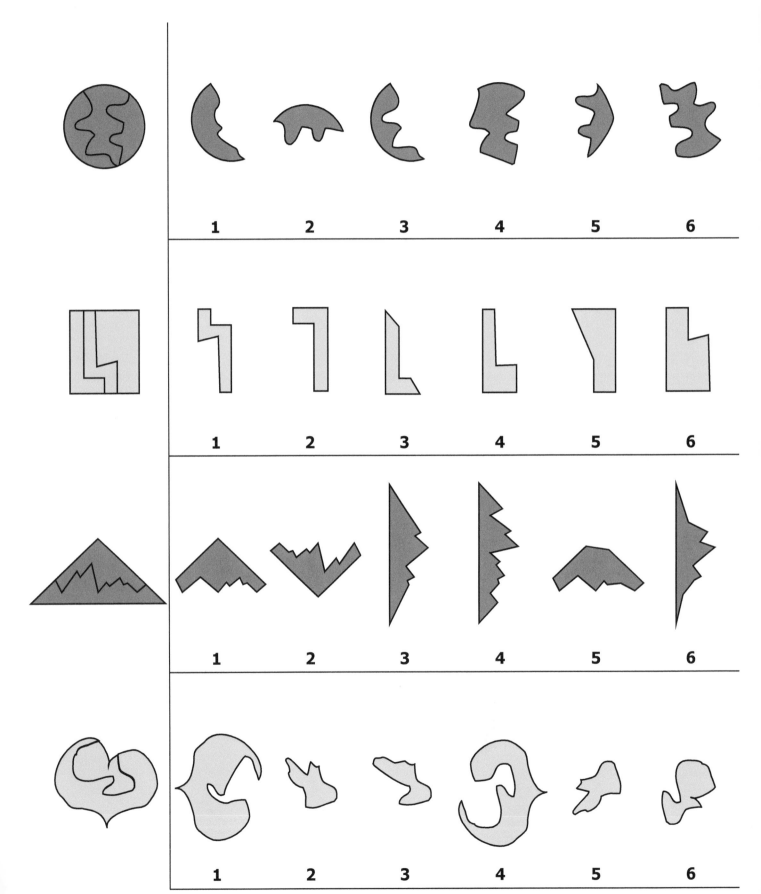

1   2   3   4   5   6

1   2   3   4   5   6

1   2   3   4   5   6

1   2   3   4   5   6

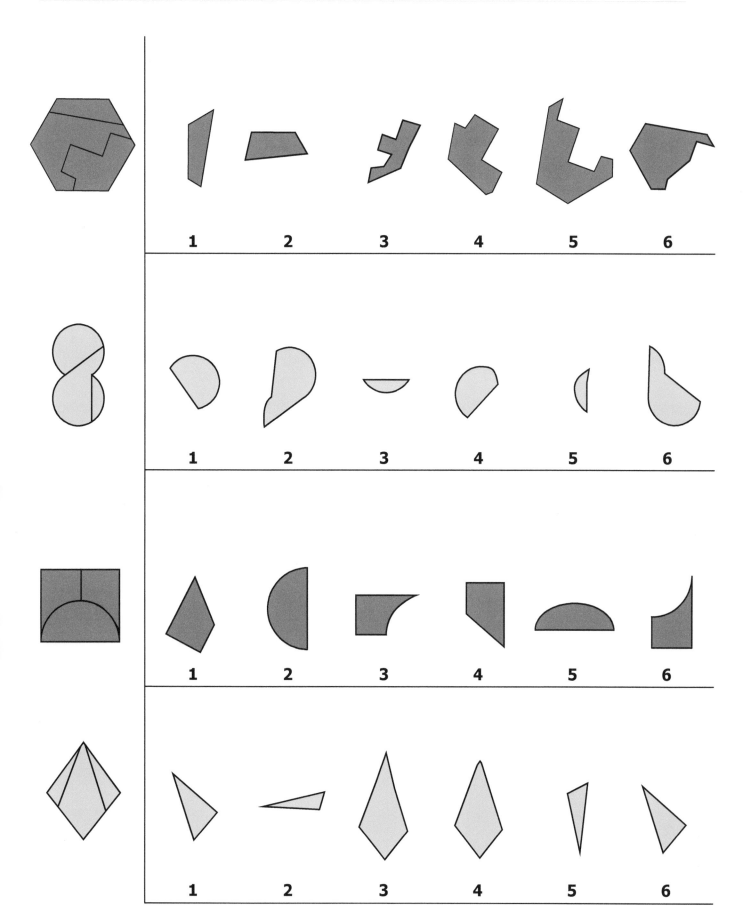

Test Tutor Publishing, LLC

11654 Plaza America Drive, #191
Reston, VA 20190

info@the-test-tutor.com
www.the-test-tutor.com
888-577-9906

CPSIA information can be obtained
at www.ICGtesting.com
Printed in the USA
BVHW022026190419
546031BV00006B/9/P